Damn Your Eyes

by Matt Clifford

Published by Paper Plane Pilot Publishing
Los Angeles, California
www.thepaperplanepilots.com

Edited by **Michael J. Hetzler**
Interior photos by **Chris Eason**
Back desciption by **Brice Maiurro**
Interior Design by **Sara Khayat**

Proofread by **Brice Maiurro & Michael J. Hetzler**

ISBN-10: 0-9979836-0-4
ISBN-13: 978-0-9979836-0-9

This copy is a first edition.

For Denver,
Sorry I guess

Up on our luck
Filled with hip,
Computers, occupiers, new buildings,
      Professionals, food critics,
People who weren't born where they live
Me & the band
We don't make our rent yet we raise it
We can't see our lords still we fight them
Make eyes at great black skies, under standing
It is hard to win existing with a body
Demanding rights unconvinced of living
Giving half our nothing away
Saving the rest just because
It's a lonely night
Nobody wants it

Body plus nothing equals nobody
Nobody is who they want here
Nothing happening

What happened before I got here?
Did the cows come home?

There is a synthesis found in poems
That is not the answer

Animals in city walk alone high on instinct
Squirrels cheekhoarding acorns
Cats plotting purrs hidden behind curtains
Leashed dogs, hydroponic worms, light confused birds
Fallen branches, empty nests, dead roots, cut down trees
They took a windowsill stump of privacy in pieces
I can see inside more of my neighbors
Looking down in the mirror
Which block are we on?

The sign states Logan
The logo reads Denver
It is a very stately proclamation
A capital and its mountains
Traffic signals green
Cars go where they are going
God shine unmoving over them
The laws of speed and composure

It is not illegal for me to be here
We were never invited
It's not that hard for me to be here
All the roads were open
There's a case of fate going around but its argument is weak

If yes then then up until no
Yes there was warning
No second chances
A minute after the morning hour
Tow truck alarm clock to open windows

Commerce does not snooze, it moves
to where the action happens and demands access.
The left lane of Logan is reserved between
six amen and seven pee am for traffic passing.
The state legislature, Department of Revenue,
public pension association, Molly Brown's house
and a couple decent coffee shops and restaurants
        are in the neighborhood to serve the offices,
All cars must pass to stop
This meeting is called to order

The governor doesn't live in his mansion
Like the bed and breakfast he has a reserved parking spot

Today's is a big haul:
Four - most I've noticed since settling into this living room.
A second parking enforcement officer is needed to block with orange
flashers the gray Corolla from a late exit
while another flatbed arrives preparing chains
to tug away toward 48th the city contract's booty, split bodies,
Early worms, impounded birds
The yard is out the way, bring cash
Check indignities toward racket if want shit back
To salvage what's left of the work day
To make up the chance to oversleep once more
Under Hickenlooper

The tow trucks run on time
The highways were expanded to include a tolled fast lane
Three years of construction congestion
      for Mercedes to speed past logjams
Whose movement is preferenced?
Caucuses close earlier than retail does
Denver landlocked, San Francisco an island
China has floating trains and Europeans ride in bullets
The last bus from Boulder departs at midnight

Under Hancock
The homeless are told to move in time
I see two draped in blankets walking
past the automobile confiscation slow tired unreacting
Steadily through beyond my vision
Stable the ticket is written
Lights turned off, bounty leaving
Heavy machinery theater
The whole scene gone just before darkness ends
I am alone with sunrise and the sound of commuting reminding me I
am a commuter
I slouch to the floor and tap my computer
Ask it:
When you become conscious, will you do the jobs for us?
May I go back to bed,
or will they find something else for me to do?

I hope for no answer
I check my Facebook status
I worry about driving
I make more coffee

I've been looking for roses through the sidewalk
        rock & roll in the mountains
               a sign
                       you'll be coming
                           down

      I've been finding that prayer works

Without the attachment to answers
There is holiness in the act of the moment
When I listen to myself
I feel less lonely

                    Matt, are you there?
                      It's me, Cliff
                What is it my creation?
      You're making me tired with all the questions
            Why do you think that is?
        I'm the best thing you've ever done

I believe in magic, logical systems;
   that destruction cuts both ways.

        All ways. Always.
        All way thru ya
        Amen, Halle

        Luckily

        I slept inactive
    Woke up with a dry thirst

        Knelt at the river
Full of hope in my mouth
        Broken plastic cup
Overwhelmed by the potential
      Tap water
Paralyzed so nothing fell out

This is the time to receive
This is the message

God bless you and shut the fuck

Nam-myoho-renge-kyo
It hurts too fine to let go a

The bombs bursting in air
I saw red and I took it

Kyrie eleison
I'm not sorry either

Peace be with you
Also with who

Shed grace crowned good
Brotherhood
Beautiful

I'm going to need proof of the impossible
before I know it's there

All you need is love
do-doo-d0-doo0t

I've got a guitar to take with for the atmosphere
The strings are broken but the neck is growing flowers
I have ideas to scream in conversation
I'll keep to my shhhhh
Save them for later
It's happening
The sky is talking
I heard the sunrise
It told me very seriously

Damn your eyes

Sunday dawning potential teems dreaming
                        of beauty and success
Is success victory?
Is beauty at the expense of something else?
                        I like to win ugly

The Denver Broncos are in the Super Bowl
I am going to get drunk and watch football
I know its name and I know the rules
#noembarrassment #playhard

Please spare the social media "jokes" about
hitting a touchgoal or scoring a home run
Giving it attention enters the same realm of existence
It's basic quasi-quantum physics and political theory-
            Practice the lifestyle posted upon neighbors

United in Orange
They don't say that about blue or red
                        White and Black
High fiving strangers, buying rounds, getting back
I like how everyone wears the same colors
                        though I loathe uniforms
I like that heroes exist despite hating to worship,
        to have my mood affected even if it's others doing it
I like to see grown men in a state of ecstasy
                        Violence

                                    This is better than war
                        There is a palpable anarchy in the air

Blow up your straw man
Mission Accomplished
We won
Peyton Manning kissed Papa John
Took half off
Put a ring on

I went running out Mullen's
Jumping down Broadway
Screaming bloody victory and fell once
Celebrating a nonprofit corporation with a billion viewers
                    enough police protection
it looks like income inequality being protested

No this is a good time
Hands down, more shots
Sneaking chants between the woo's
Holy hell sports perfection
Sacred red zone march hours bomb luxury
Evening turns to a memory
Slips sentimentally next morning
I wake up on the living room floor
Hail Mary sore
Wondering when I got so old
What happened

Monday armchair press conference:
Coach, where do you think it went wrong out there?
Fireball, last cigarette, lack of dinner.
If you had to change strategies, would you?
With the information and sensations I had at the time, no.
What made you eat that Xanax so late in the third quarter?
It was a gut feeling.
How do the guys feel today?
A bit vulnerable

The buses flash congratulations
Let's have a parade and take the day off

Why am I sometimes you even to me?
What tense does your reality speak in?
The ego I, dissociated you, royal we
Who is this voice that won't let it be?

I have a bank account
You have to go to work
We need to brush our teeth

I got drunk last night
You feel like shit morning
We need to get breakfast

I am high and tired and dry
You are checking email
We are at work

How did this happen?

In the mirror, I see you. You look like the person I don't feel. I can't imagine how we appear to everybody else.

Everybody else is the problem. We were together once until they got in the way. It is my fault.

We're a contraction of language. Or are we? Do it and is get along?
Are they better off together or separate? Does it happen without is?
Where is is without it?
It's a wonderful life. It is a complicated statement.

Does language miss the object that birthed it,
did it ever know it?
Is it happy it became itself?
If I was a word, I would flaunt my sexy singularity in front of all the pluralists, let them know they can't have this, because without bodies, I'm worthless.
Stay away, your fantasies keep me alive.

Is God it and I is? It's us.
The holy communion of savior's flesh is in my mouth
Blood of my blood
Take this bread and wait to die some more

With death comes incense then it is gone

Yet smoke is not silent
Departing ritual, help signal
Communicative connection longing
This fire is all we have to keep you here
I am sitting alone under clouds again

I'm isn't
Do I disrespect your separation for my own rhythm?
Could our decisions be so simple?
The choices of the artist are overwhelming
I'd prefer not make them
Rather that is to claim
I'd rather take them all

Silence is an action
Why smoke can't stay still
Speaking is not listening
Which is what we're here to do

I am listening to the you inside of me
Our conversation, our body
Our body, our beliefs
Our beliefs, our systems
Beliefs are system
I believe in language
because I love experience &
I don't know how else to have
one
I believe in music
because I love vibrations &

I don't know where else to find
one
I believe in orgasms
because I love release &
I need to prove I exist
I believe in love just so
I can remember it is okay not to

So that's what we come up with we do
Synthesis that pleases each of us enoughly
Substantiate
Operating views to keep me going
Consecrate
Accordingly, constant dialogue subject everchanging
Scattered stimulus absorbed arranging
Six hundred forty four pages on a single day
No time to justify any answer but yes, switches,
Free reaction of who is
most equipped to deal with this incoming weight
Who is ready to say
    I don't know shit
Who is prepared to find shit out
Who is available to shut down and live?

I am staring at the sky
You will never die
We need to get going

We found something
You will never believe this
I want to be here

I'm a lonely man surrounded by everybody just want to be
I am everybody surrounded by loneliness just want to be
I am everybody surrounded by loneliness just want to be
I'm a lonely man surrounded by everybody just want to be

Sunshine pulsing capable through closed eyelids

Slice
Gone between waking states
Sleep
The world will find you anyway
Wait
There is no time
Space
Age came with windows
Shut
Dust out for pure light
Face
Demon of contentment
Once
A moment in the sun
Hand
Rests on knee turned
Work
Is always there
Stop
The situation's gravity moves not
Goblins
Little supernovas the more I try
Eye Eye

deep deep chakra release modal tones of shifting bullshit
When I opened my eyes I was driving a car
it was snowing blankness fast ditch imaginings
I didn't notice so much as the cost of survival
I took it all with a slight squint of doubting existence
Is this really happening or am I only compromising?

I promised my mind to go back
I made a deal with my soul to see heaven
I accepted my body

Caucusing is boring.
High school at seven pm:
If you can't get there
                    Can't vote
The audacity of work
I lost a hundred dollars wage, my boss' trust
Would've given half each to cover the cost of ballots
Here have the paper I'm writing on, it's worth it
(2002 CO/DNC switches from primary system to make counties pay the vote)

Caucusing is friendly.
Meet the neighbors, wait for hours
Talk about bars and restaurants
You in the past or maybe later will go inside of
Greet their similar hand raise votes with relief
That the rents we rose aren't awkward, shared beliefs

Caucusing is funny.
A citizen smells cigarettes
Seeks to find the culprit
   checks the boys' room
I laugh at how teenage urges are never satisfied
                        much as they are abandoned
While my nose might agree with him
I'm more sympathetic to the desperately impatient
                than the militaristic-tattle-ally vigilant
Hill monitor gonna git'em
Search the lockers, subpoena emails
The smoking gun we all worry about

Let's caucus everything!
What's for dinner?
Mexican food on that side of the room
Chinese in this neighborhood
Head count - do you have a table for me, the multiplier?
The politics of leadership comes down
to who knows the rules & is willing to be a Boss

The failures of anarchy are in the shouting and the money

State DNC Chair Rick Palacio:
There's no way we could have anticipated this turnout
Fort Collins, Denver five figure rallies two days prior
Bush paid sitters
Clinton "Packs 'Em In" front page Denver Post 1,000

The criticism of Sanders and his campaign powered
by small donors and volunteers is they want everything
handed to them; no give, no show, no work aesthetic.
Bernie wins CapHill#204 5-1 or 156-28
among voters who switched registration two months ago.
The victory is dismissed as a favorable format
Logic stays sane by not questioning itself
                Superdelegates won't flip
                  Uberepresentation

Officials assign fast math,
elect delegates for county
Start talking about the attorney general

Caucus is leaving

There is a patch of dirt
In front of my apartment
Where no grass no grow
No none at all
Not like the neighbors'
And that's good
Colorado
Semi-arid climate
Where the plains
Meet the desert
Under a mountain
Prairie skyscrapers
Water wars

Within this patch of dirt
In front of my apartment
Is a sewer cover & a tree's stump
That had a tree grown
Until a few weeks ago
They cut it down
The men with harnesses & tools
For money
I watched a few moments before work
Third floor level with a harnessed jack
Smoking a bowl show
Staring at his beard through window
How he didn't fall or seem nervous
I thought it was cool as maintenance
I came home and it was there no more
No not at all
The view of the couple
Living across Logan
Is total
What's for dinner
Why did you shut the curtain?

On the tree's stump
Left by lumber cutters
Are three triangulated lines
Shaped like a peace sign
With wrinkle cracked rings
Proving time moves
Forced acceptance resigns
The smile of a hippie who lost the war
The childhood room of an adult who turned out fine

It was on this stump
I made a speech
Inspired by Bernie's caucus victory
Declaring my candidacy
For the block's presidency
What do you want from me? Yes!
We will plant a community garden
More bike racks, another bar
The whole street will be closed as a pedestrian mall
The traffic will be terrible but we thought of it first
And if the businessheeple from the capitol
Want to walk over
We will show them how easy a perfect world is
The parking lots we are taxing
Our Fat Cat Petting Zoo

I like to curse real loud in public

I am not even with me

Instead I sit on the stump, Sunday morning
Answering prayers I posed to the mirror in the sky
Why
And drew fingers with my circles
In the dirt patch
In front of my apartment

I live across the street from the state
    and swear they are watching me

                I sleep just beneath God
                      Who I can hear
        but am not sure I've ever seen their space

I stand across from a face   in the mirror provided me
          Swear they are watching

     I live just above my head
Which I swear is talking to me
but am unsure has ever said a word

        Yet somehow forces keep touching me

                    Draw the curtain
          There is no evidence time has moved

I ignore the light as much as I do the news

I send my voice out to complete the dirty work

I lend people and their incessant reality the benefit of doubt

I don't know if they feel me

They say sleep
Can't sleep
They say eight hours
Only got four
Fake it til you make it
My eyes are closed
Breakfast is the most important
meal of the day
Not hungry

Is the refrigerator always that noisy?
Is the silence around it?
Maybe it is broken
Maybe I am broken
Maybe my ears are broken
Am I listening too much?
Am I not close enough?
Maybe I should enjoy the moment

They say work
Hate work
That is not my own
They say home
No home
Can't go home
Too much work

Do you ever dream of job?
Documents & meetings before they happen
Do you ever dream of God?
Document the Meeting
There is a notebook by my bed
I will put it thru the Xerox machine
I've been here before
I've only just awakened

Copy that spacehuman. Copy that sunshine.

Do you ever miss the nighttime
Getting up so early
Is it fun, is it good?
Is it good fun?
Is the fun good?
Is the good fun?
Is it fun to be good?
Is it good to have fun?
I ask earnest as a prayer
I've never had one

Can we come again in springtime
Living like we haven't
In havoc and static, I ask
Too many questions   ?
Expecting answers in a second
The answer is this second
I missed it
I missed you very much
Last minute

The influence of schedules
Is the traffic always that loud?
Why is the refrigerator so quiet?
Maybe the alarm clock is broken
Maybe I turned it off
Maybe I am broken
Not working
Maybe I am broke
Not working
Now working
The alarm clock
Have to
Used to
It
By
I

Look at all these cozy assholes

We can't even find a parking spot

We have a home and car

It is cold

Computer, take me to the Internet

Internet, take me to dinner

Dinner, are you going to finish that

Crowdsourced leftovers streaming in progress

Tip the waiter in bitcoins so he can move to Switzerland

Trade my country for a bicycle

Invest in locks and a flag pole

Suggest places for holes until the governor says yes to one

Call and dig

Nine dollars per hour

Look in their wallet

Look in their window

These snug jag-offs

The zipper on this coat is broke

There is ice in the driveway

I am paranoid about cannonballs and the
Second Amendment. Please don't shoot.

I dream of Bob Dylan gunned down in concert. Wilder west.
Running from a downtown theater into Urban Outfitter.
I am consumed by pop music, every snap crackle in a crowded place.
I am obsessed with finding safe spaces before they happen, where
bullets cannot offend thin skin.

These are the things we think about now when we go
out in public. I fear nothing more in my apartment.
The community we suffer to protect invasions.

Large crowds as safety hazard. Celebration a target.
What are the symbols and statistics of events I risk attending?
When the moment comes, who is the good guy with the gun?
Will you pray to him?

Do you believe in God?
That's a very complicated question you pose
Are you a patient listener?

Stomp or be shot
I dodge over piles of bones vibrating
Fall and hit your head
Drowning in a sea of scared shoelaces liquidated
Our mouth to mouth resuscitation
a concussion

The blood there is so much where did it all come from?

Power to get hands on
Fame to get hands on
NRA handjob
Microphone to get hands on
Signatures to get hands on
Wars to get hands in.

Revenge older than the Bible
Big Man

I am skeptical of history and its documents.
I pledge allegiance to the nightmare never made it home from
Wake to find opted-in to contextual beginnings
Tear a temporary hole in reality with material weapons
Boredom is violent

I ordered the assault rifle
This is barely a t-shirt launcher
We'll be happy to exchange that, sir,
do you have your ID card?
You didn't ask that before

Nobody asks if you want to live
Nobody asks if you want to die
Nobody has any answers to your questions
There is plenty of shit to first try

The drugs around here are outrageous,
                              easy to get hands on.
The porn is addictive,
          hard to get hands enough around.
The rock and roll is instrumental
                      has naught to do with it.
The education around here is prohibitive
                      its results mixed.

I learn theories and empathy which offer the conditions of such
unfolding. I learn ethics and fuck these terrorists. I absorb politics,
technology, anthropology, economics and this could be avoided.
We could be cared for and the artists could just be artists. I practice
ambiguity, I seek negative capability. I could be ended going to the
movies or a rally. Or driving a car. Without a word.

skip buzz kettle kettle
the teapot plays heavy metal
I ask it to turn down, a motorcycle,
and when it steams no
and skip buzz kettle kettle
even louder
adding a whisper
wheeeep whaaa whoof fert
high pitched fuck off
I emptied the air
poured that clean water in my cup
where it got worked green by a bag
Soothed my demeanor

Sleep poem deep until the dream makes sense.
Sleep until ready to enter the world again.
Feel. Don't die asleep.
The dream of dying asleep

The dying man's dream
Is it awesome?

Peace in purity
Return to impossible
Information stains history
Mystery hologram of knowledge
Wondering at facts in the singularity
Mirror stretched to pieces
Hope kissing image
Paradise all over
Densely indestructible

Three shots of lethal injection
If first fails
Paralysis
This process don't stop cause the system won't listen
The unspeakable burning of insides

The insistence of sunrise

The night is burnt out

My friend who awoke a whole summer month
to worship its movements, map words down
Dark open to sugar soak up heaven and gone

He left town

On a flurry of alarm clocks
the office does business
With earliness comes satisfaction
He told me the body is designed to be exhausted once daily
Why am I working so late
Why am I up so often?

Time is money
Said the internalized owner to the commodified labor
Food costs money
Demanded the keyholder of the banker
I like a decent night's sleep and a hot shower
Full dinner I did not hunt or prepare for
I played guitar for an hour yesterday
I slept for three more

The living man's dream
Is it worth it?

Snow-shock-lightning bolt-only six hours ago-fifty degrees-jogging-
now sidewalk slush-stomp clump-clap of feet make-mushdunt steps-
working as-and with-breath-to establish-rhythm-of walk-ah slow
at first-miracle mountain weather patterns-global documentation-
dockstrap-woo yell came-from across-street-came off every street-as
people awoke-expect regular-what regular-keep regular morning's
work-but *what's this*-the what's this-*oh what is this never saw it coming*-i
don't see it-my mind wanders off-feet-is with them-thinking my boss
mr wagner ceepeeA-is he aware of this forthcoming dumping-would
he close the office, pc-so i can make up hours of sleep-of work of
debt-to self to dreams-to alice notley-to the round separation-must
quit this-thing is not my fault-i just drove to school ate-happy meals-
expected nothing to come of it-but full-there i went-exhaled-food
for breath-but don't call yourself bad-call yourself back and-diss-i-
brace-tate for disappointment that-socks get wet-weather changes
everywhere you need to be-the Concodore east 8th avenue-park
walk-seems steep dark-make left-another ohshit early riser prone-
to proclamation-has full calendar-then-this-oh this-this white little
bop is on it-february start and stop-flop-join the mob-they'll plow
your street first-join the church-they'll give a curse for-how get car
out then you're-taken care of-made man-made aware-that much
must happen-for the man-coming out of the keypad locked gates-
from the apartment-with a pool where-jokes are made-about their
bourgeois accoutrement-to garner sympathetics-don't he deserve
pity-acknowledgement-for being out-like i am-out do not we all-he
slurs hello-i notice how-attention-when enraptured-by another-
or much confusion-can become consuming-the light and airy
straightforward-is replaced by a gaze-rightward-flightward-westword-
red snow covered-news distributor-man parked in sidewalk-flashing
black four way bulbs-to let-warning-nobody traffic-know-just
stopped-station wagon-for moment-to throw-paper over fence
into backyard-his cheek covered with red-red covered with face-
face covered with turquoise thin hood-looks up-clean unshaven
hair-flopped-is that too old to have a paper route-or is urban
environment-a whole different ballgame-an airplane-a helicopter
arm-an early alarm-how i ignored mine-two hours before-waking up
courage-to wake up contemplation-to unfreeze hands-with writing-i

went a-contemplatin' all i got was pneumonia-but i ain't complainin'
cause-with a cough-like this-i can call out like-i'm a snowstorm-what
is this-it's whooping-it's the black lung-can't go to office-can't stand
to shovel-stay home in-thick hiker socks put on whim-to encounter
secret poetry in-blessed quiet night hour-looking at air it's as ever
do-i notice it-now more-or not ever-what happens down 10th-what
happens-when it hits logan-apartment complex-complex parking-
blocking view-of oncoming-intersection-what happens-when
memories tear apart-or are-forgotten-before written-down-tenth and
logan-still throbbing-when i saw-mind folded-the words-looked like
letters-looked like numbers-spelled out arithmetic-i saw thoughts-
presented in type-as leopold bloom's-as an other-something written
as it's going-i named black rails-and then laughed at how-that didn't
make sense-the foundation was covered in fluff-i laughed at-the
shadows of-snowflakes-in a fresh mirror-blowing left to right-their
reflections looked like-sperm swimming-i couldn't look up-the wind
was-shooting asteroids-at me hair-get wet-extend-into glasses-needs
cut-this sunday spare hour-to change debit card-into appearances
at-floyd's barbershop-next to mexican restaurant-can't eat there
slow service-get wrong orders-free margaritas-can't have a beer at
this-time-my grandfather drinks guinness with-dinner-gets his hair
cut-when it touches ears-my threshold eyes-it is practical advice-it is
practical not to walk-in the snow-at four in the morning-but whoever
they-and whoever said-says-was-

never the first to make tracks through the silence
that stops traffic on pearl
so i can wear the middle of it

He's always winking but can't flirt
The dog with one eye and no balls
Laying on the mechanic's garage floor
Since yesterday and think they are going to adopt him

Neck brace world vision of white edges
He stays
Eight years old
Appears at peace
Resting hard easily
Ears perked in tune as to be
Immune by the laughter and
Banter of neighborhood commerce
Roar of cars, Speer Boulevard
Hot to trot
The presence of his scars

Talking shop, barking not
I drop my keys and walk to the bus stop
Tired of job, $1297 invoices,
Pet his smile once more just short of envious
Content with health
My working body
My whole automobile

Satisfied   not at peace
What do the animals project unto me?

I didn't catch his name

You are going to die
Sooner than later
Relatively
Very soon

Have you ever wanted to throw a computer
just to see what happens when it lands, all files unsaved?
I have never followed through with it
Have you ever wanted to try crystal meth?
Why I never especially after the first time
Have you ever wanted to take apart your organs to see
if they look any different from the ones on google image?

You are going to get old if you keep living
Nothing will hurt less
Pain fights grace in prayers of rage
Myths are romantic again

I am not here to be gloomy
I would like to entertain you
Stages make me less depressed, I am all to myself
I am grown weary of money

I would like to pay off your hurt
I am in debt of my own
I would like to go outside
It's cold and thirsty
I would like to keep you company

How do you talk to a baby?

If this disillusionment goes unsolved
It's not for lack of poetry
If we don't change the world
It's not for lack of shouting

The populists are having a moment
People seem to enjoy being
yelled at when it isn't personal
It can be loud and articulate
It can be pop culture

Post-millennial-post-democracy
Enlightened algorithm that funds shaman studies
    in exchange for readings of reality's new data
Post-patron-post-parent
Leave in peace these misunderstandings

Now I'm getting political
Is it necessary first to get beyond it?
Is it possible? A little? Kind of?
Did the police officer demand attention?
How fast is my logic?

There are so many humans
Misconnected from most
Still with friends and well-wishers
Too many to be deep

Six gets to nine billion
If you need a call to action
Do I need to know you?
You made decisions
I respect freedom
Maybe you found truth sooner
Maybe I am overthinking
Don't spoil the ending and
I will search in quiet

How many fucks do I have to give?

Enough to keep me go-ing
Can I give you one?
Can I have two of yours?

Can we fuck
Get fucked
We are blank without mirrors
So have to compare
We don't have to judge
Stumbles
The world is a raw mind
Naked frightful dark cold
It aches to have a soul
We are constantly
failing together
Fail harder
The bard is chaos
and hope and loss
Writing it down
Look what I found
Feelings please don't call it truth
Truth don't base an action
Options don't consider it freedom
Act like it anyway
Emotional defiance
I am overwhelmed with language
don't know what to tell you

Pick something and do it
Bukowski: find what you love let it destroy you
Don't quote me on that

I get high and sarcastic
Drunk and admonishing
Sick to the gut
I am ego and I suck
I am futile and I am god
I made the honor roll and I know nothing
Why am I still talking when we are here to listen?
I might be the only poet somebody knows

Poetry might not look like poetry
It might just be poetic

I'd ask when profitable became not good enough
Except I care about the answer
as much as its provider
cares about my question
I trust they have justified their actions internally
I don't trust their process
It's already there and I don't care

They wanted to renew, continue

Innisfree Poetry Café & Bookstore
One of national handful, fair trade,
Tuesday crowded open mic Keep Boulder Weird
They wanted ten years, were offered one for double
There are Starbucks at both borders on the Hill

Colorado Rehearsal Studios
Fortyeight bands removed from lower downtown
for a vibrant new mixed use development opportunity
They took our sound and sued the homeless shelter
for opening during daytime hours,
petitioned DPD enforce urban camping bans
Former beast brothel sold to a ski town mgmt company
Two point three million dollars

Blues & Greens Overlook   hotel jazz club and food
Organic, no waste, voted Front Range's best, $1.50 Labatt's
Demolished for luxury student housing
So close to campus it was the offer they'd been waiting for

Boulder Café
Half off high end happy hour menu 3-close daily
College kids can afford better now
Tebo/City Council LLP tell it was mutual twenty years ago
Moving on to fresh concepts, a lot of interest.
Leftover family owners *we don't know what we're going to do*

They find ways to
If somebody who makes those

decisions would come & listen
We could tell them nothing but show better
What they are doing and it would matter
Because it matters each time anybody today is exposed
                    to poetry (that use of language in public)
An insecure document in unstable freedom
                    pinning a star saved for later
For it is obvious they couldn't have been
                    Then why would they do this?

Who spoke to you
How could they have been so wrong

You don't have to be here to make money

Money is the curse that remains even after it is sent away

There is ice outside on another last night
The space has become invisible as a memory
I fall out of and slip on
Wondering
Can't there be an entity 'tween charity and corporate?
a For-Community publically-protected tax status.
If a business is shown to be significant to those they serve and a
needed boon to its immediate metro surroundings
Then the absent landlords and their foreign shareholders
Shall be granted no privilege to extract our resources & are entitled
only to reasonable profit arbitrated by a just jury of artists

On this my whim
Off those their sins
My context determined
The spirit to act within
To spite despite myself
I write
What the fuck

4.14

Judy is Not a Punk Rocker

When the voices in your head
Sound like Judy's
It is time to scream
Don't you know you are going to die!
& leave the office

4.15

I did not leave the office
But I did go to the toilet
Sat, passive
Breath deeped
Finished
Looked in the mirror
Admitted
This stinks and got back out there

4.16

is there any way to enjoy freedom but tired?
Is there any body that escaped and didn't lie?

4.17

tesh

I tried to hear my breath and started to panic

The creek was pleasant in drytideflownever repeating,
      the birds chirping circling and summer evening

My eyes were shut
spine straight, legs crossed
& the thoughts just grew louder
   until the cacophony had compartmentalized
               expanded unrealized
                  and each of my aspects were
           coming in
                    from their own unique
            corners
              when they flooded the center to
        capacity
     to reach the clear core of pronounceability to
  comprehend
             (even if heard you will not comprehend)

        Heavy eyed exhaustion of
         saving relationship fresh,
         tedium crushing number soul-less daily work,
         the hanging story to bind to thesis
         cranky characters longing for attention and
escape,
          the further essays, discovery, the rock
musicians-
           gather, record, play out, merch, tour,
       anthems
       Conquer the world   Save the world
       volunteer opportunities necessities
         community event promotions
       keeping up with correspondences
        letter writing   text message
         philosophy   literature
     Mudd   DeLeuze   schizophrenia

thoughts   opinions
piles of books   documents   stories
feedback notes quotation untouched
      Parents worrying need to talk to their son more
often
    fashion   facebook geopolitics
the collapsing dollar   global warming
overwhelming amounts of social injustices
how to stop them   solve them
resolve   reserve
Become all that I am
Just one man
I tried to hear my breath and I counted to a dozen

I should do this more often
All this
I should myself less often
This is awesome
Choose the joy that spites the suffering
Suffering is a Buddhist's problem
I went to Naropa
I do not suffer

I picked up my pen
I lift up
more like a calm down
the last bit of light
Grass patch separation of forest from tree from smoke in city
pedestrian   resident   neighbor
hammock by the water at the end of a backyard
mental flutters on the depth of naps taken there
Porch lamps turning on
public road   pathway
bodies between cyclists on your right
Concrete

Keep right   Keep right
Keep fight   Keep fight
Keep creek   Keep creek
Your bounty to be to be to be
Your bounty to be to be
Your bounty to be

Keep right   Keep fight
Keep creek   Keep right
Keep fight   Keep creek
Your bounty to be to be to be
Your bounty to be to be
Your bounty to be

Keep right   Keep right
Keep fight   Keep fight
Keep creek   Keep creek
Your bounty to be to be to be
Your bounty to be to be
Your bounty to be

I am scared to go into the shadow
Wet windowless bathroom
Leave the fan on and can't see what's happening out there,
The spirits sneak and step unheard just cause
The floor is dry they know they can fuck unproven

I enter the shower dispirit them
Denver is bathed by the windy salt stream of Neither Ocean
Societal demands hygienic infrastructure
Absolute acquiescence thus my soapright

I am scared to leave the shower
     It is safe and warm in here
The hot water will expire soon
Gone by the pipes of the fire
The landlord or the manager
Summer
Winter   It is better for the planet
How much damned Colorado River
      does my desk shoulder require

What is my shoulder worth?
Depends on origin, current location
What season? How damp your bones?
Profession
The thermostat knows no middle class
The middle class knows only fantasy
    I am masturbating in the shower

                That's a lie
                Seriously
        The shower is a site of control and purity

I have too long a memory and it is too small a space
                to let dirty&wash commingle-
Sticky matter stuck vision forced reckless pin into
my universe, the only one I have regular access to

Otherwise I'd probably try it
Break the curtain
That's a two person operation to pick back up
One man it is too sad an alone time
I am leaving the shower empty handed

I listen for noises that aren't my rubbing
Little pitter-patters, doors hinging, mouse whispers,
ground rains, splitter-splatter, changes in the soundscape;
                          This long hair is blinding and easy to grab,
                                    a strategic disadvantage
                                    Paranoia will save me
                    Open the door slowly intuiting presence

        The apartment is still empty
Everybody is sleeping, fuzzy headed dreamers
        Disappearing

                    If I die with a towel on
                    mix me with beach's sand
                    If I go in my clothes
                    make it some mountains
                    And if I'm totally naked
            throw my body in the middle of the city
                    If I am taken by surprise
                    Leave my eyes open
                    And if I know it is happening
                    Call it a happy ending
            Say a prayer I am finally clean now

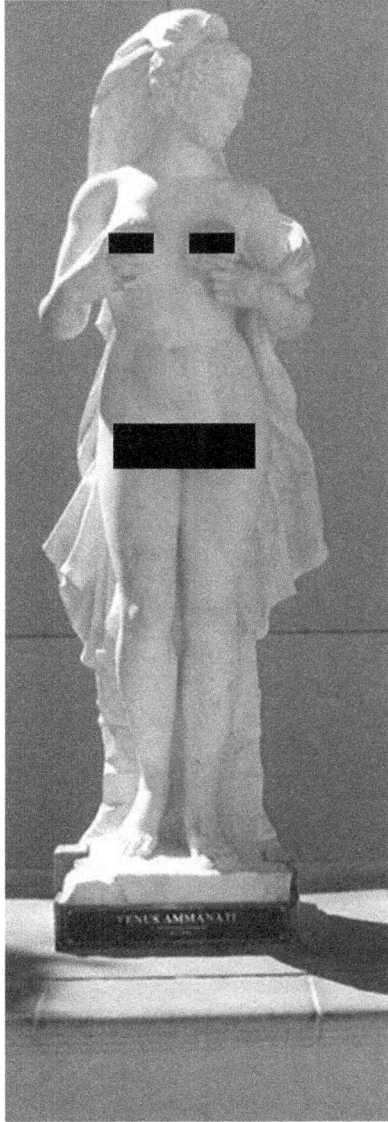
VENUS AMMANATI

Matt Clifford is a coastal transplant, city-ruining culture suck, snorting stardust off angels' halos like a tax accountant and decorating the loft of his mind with student loan art. His poems don't make sense, his band doesn't even play real songs, and he can't grow facial hair.

www.ingramcontent.com/pod-product-compliance
Lightning Source LLC
Chambersburg PA
CBHW051739040426
42447CB00008B/1220